M000079481

MOM IN A MILLION

This edition copyright © Summersdale Publishers Ltd, 2019
First edition published as *Bestest Mum Ever* in 2011
Second edition published as *Best Mum Ever* in 2016

Heart icon © daisybee/Shutterstock.com

All rights reserved.

No part of this book may be reproduced by any means, nor transmitted, nor translated into a machine language, without the written permission of the publishers.

Condition of Sale
This book is sold subject to the condition that it shall not, by way of trade or otherwise, be lent, resold, hired out or otherwise circulated in any form of binding or cover other than that in which it is published and without a similar condition including this condition being imposed on the subsequent purchaser.

An Hachette UK Company
www.hachette.co.uk

Summersdale Publishers Ltd
Part of Octopus Publishing Group Limited
Carmelite House
50 Victoria Embankment
LONDON
EC4Y 0DZ

www.summersdale.com

Printed and bound in China

ISBN: 978-1-78685-755-2

Substantial discounts on bulk quantities of Summersdale books are available to corporations, professional associations and other organizations. For details contact general enquiries: telephone: +44 (0) 1243 771107 or email: enquiries@summersdale.com.

MOM
— IN A —
MILLION

summersdale

TO ....

FROM..........................

A mother's love for her
child is like nothing
else in the world.

- AGATHA CHRISTIE -

IF EVOLUTION REALLY
WORKS, HOW COME
MOTHERS ONLY HAVE
TWO HANDS?

- MILTON BERLE -

A MOM IS A FRIEND
WHO WILL NEVER
LEAVE YOU.

A MOTHER
UNDERSTANDS
WHAT A CHILD
DOES NOT SAY.

- JEWISH PROVERB -

ANY MOTHER
COULD PERFORM
THE JOBS
**OF SEVERAL
AIR-TRAFFIC
CONTROLLERS
WITH EASE.**

- LISA ALTHER -

THINGS THAT MOMS CAN DO WITH ONE HAND TIED BEHIND THEIR BACK:

Organize the week ahead
for the entire family—
pets included!

Hang out a load of laundry
while ironing the last batch

Bake culinary treats
for any occasion

Get the old family photo albums out and open to the baby pictures before your visitors have even sat down

A MOTHER IS ONE TO WHOM YOU HURRY WHEN YOU ARE TROUBLED.

- EMILY DICKINSON -

MY MOTHER IS A
WALKING MIRACLE.

- LEONARDO DiCAPRIO -

WE HAVE CHARTS,
MAPS, AND LISTS
ON THE FRIDGE, ALL
OVER THE HOUSE. I
SOMETIMES FEEL LIKE
I'M WITH THE CIA.

- KATE WINSLET -

THERE IS NO WAY
TO BE A PERFECT
MOTHER, **AND A**
MILLION WAYS TO
BE A GOOD ONE.

- JILL CHURCHILL -

My mother taught me that there are more valuable ways to achieve beauty than just through your external features.

- LUPITA NYONG'O -

I THINK YOU
ARE PRETTY MUCH
PERFECT, IN
EVERY WAY!

A MOTHER'S HEART IS A PATCHWORK OF LOVE.

- ANONYMOUS -

THE ART OF
MOTHERING IS TO
TEACH THE ART OF
LIVING TO CHILDREN.

- ELAINE HEFFNER -

If men had babies,
they would only
have one each.

- DIANA, PRINCESS OF WALES -

I APPRECIATE
EVERYTHING
YOU DO FOR ME.

"

**WHERE THERE IS A
MOTHER IN THE HOME,
MATTERS GO WELL.**

- AMOS BRONSON ALCOTT -

THE NATURAL STATE
OF MOTHERHOOD
IS UNSELFISHNESS.

- JESSICA LANGE -

IF LOVE IS SWEET
AS A FLOWER,
THEN MY MOTHER
IS THAT SWEET
FLOWER OF LOVE.

- STEVIE WONDER -

YOU KNOW YOU'RE A MOM WHEN...

... you can rustle up a feast from leftovers in the refrigerator

... you realize you now sound
like your own mom

... you always look slightly
disheveled while your
child looks immaculate

... you can carry five bags of groceries, your child, and your child's bike home without getting out of breath!

WHEN A CHILD
NEEDS A MOTHER
TO TALK TO,
**NOBODY ELSE
BUT A MOTHER
WILL DO.**

- ERICA JONG -

NOTHING WILL EVER
MAKE YOU AS HAPPY
OR AS SAD, AS PROUD
OR AS TIRED.

- ELIA PARSONS ON BEING A MOM -

YOU ALWAYS
FORGIVE ME.

ALL MOTHERLY LOVE
IS REALLY WITHOUT
REASON AND LOGIC.

- JOAN CHEN -

For most exhausted moms, their idea of "working out" is a good, energetic lie-down.

- KATHY LETTE -

BEAUTIFUL AS
WAS MAMMA'S
FACE, IT BECAME
INCOMPARABLY
MORE LOVELY
WHEN SHE SMILED,
AND SEEMED TO
ENLIVEN EVERYTHING
ABOUT HER.

- LEO TOLSTOY -

THERE IS NO RECIPROCITY.
MEN LOVE WOMEN,
WOMEN LOVE CHILDREN,
CHILDREN LOVE HAMSTERS.

- ALICE THOMAS ELLIS -

YOU ARE THE GLUE
THAT HOLDS US
ALL TOGETHER.

"

MY MOTHER MADE A BRILLIANT IMPRESSION UPON MY CHILDHOOD LIFE. SHE SHONE FOR ME LIKE THE EVENING **STAR**.

- WINSTON CHURCHILL -

There is no velvet so
soft as a mother's lap,
no rose so lovely as her
smile, no path so flowery
as that imprinted
with her footsteps.

- EDWARD THOMSON -

YOU INSPIRE ME
TO BE THE BEST
I CAN BE.

MAKING THE DECISION
TO HAVE A CHILD... IS
TO DECIDE FOREVER
TO HAVE YOUR HEART
GO WALKING AROUND
OUTSIDE YOUR BODY.

- ELIZABETH STONE -

I SHALL NEVER
FORGET MY MOTHER,
FOR IT WAS SHE
WHO PLANTED AND
NURTURED THE FIRST
SEEDS OF GOOD
WITHIN ME.

- IMMANUEL KANT -

WHEN YOU ARE
A MOTHER, **YOU
ARE NEVER REALLY
ALONE IN YOUR
THOUGHTS.**

- SOPHIA LOREN -

YOU ALWAYS
SUPPORT ME.

TO DESCRIBE MY
MOTHER WOULD BE
TO WRITE ABOUT A
HURRICANE IN ITS
PERFECT POWER.

- MAYA ANGELOU -

A MOTHER'S ARMS
ARE MADE OF
TENDERNESS AND
CHILDREN SLEEP
SOUNDLY IN THEM.

- VICTOR HUGO -

THINGS THAT MAKE MOMS CRY:

First burp, first word, first steps—first anything, really!

Getting breakfast in bed on
Mother's Day—who cares
if the toast is cold?!

When someone else does
the dishes for a change

Seeing their teenager all
dressed up for the school prom—
amazing what a bit of soap
and water can do, isn't it?!

Weddings—it doesn't matter
who's getting married!

A mother's love...
perceives no
impossibilities.

- CORNELIA PADDOCK -

SWEATER, N.:
GARMENT WORN
BY CHILD WHEN
ITS MOTHER IS
FEELING CHILLY.

- AMBROSE BIERCE -

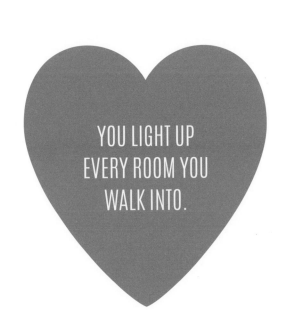

YOU LIGHT UP
EVERY ROOM YOU
WALK INTO.

"

THE GOD TO WHOM
LITTLE BOYS SAY THEIR
PRAYERS HAS A FACE
VERY LIKE THEIR
MOTHER'S.

- J. M. BARRIE -

"

IT SEEMS TO ME THAT
MY MOTHER WAS THE
MOST SPLENDID WOMAN
I EVER KNEW.

- CHARLIE CHAPLIN -

Who ran to help me
when I fell, And would
some pretty story tell,
Or kiss the place to make
it well? My mother.

- ANN TAYLOR -

SHE WOULD HAVE
DESPISED THE MODERN
IDEA OF WOMEN BEING
EQUAL TO MEN. EQUAL,
INDEED! SHE KNEW THEY
WERE SUPERIOR.

- ELIZABETH GASKELL -

THANK YOU FOR
TEACHING ME THAT I CAN
BE BOTH STRONG
AND GENTLE.

CHILDREN AND ZIP
FASTENERS DO
NOT RESPOND TO
FORCE... EXCEPT
OCCASIONALLY.

- KATHARINE WHITEHORN -

MOTHER'S LOVE IS BLISS, IS PEACE. IT NEED NOT BE ACQUIRED, IT NEED NOT BE DESERVED.

- ERICH FROMM -

MY MOTHER HAD A GOOD DEAL OF TROUBLE WITH ME, BUT I THINK SHE ENJOYED IT.

- MARK TWAIN -

I WOULDN'T SWAP
YOU FOR ANYTHING
IN THE WORLD.

I CANNOT TELL HOW
MUCH I OWE TO THE
SOLEMN WORDS OF
MY GOOD MOTHER.

- CHARLES SPURGEON -

Mother is far too clever
to understand anything
she does not like.

- ARNOLD BENNETT -

THE MOTHER'S
HEART IS THE CHILD'S
CLASSROOM.

- HENRY WARD BEECHER -

THINGS THAT ONLY
A MOM CAN TEACH:

Religion—"You'd better pray
that comes out in the wash..."

Medical science—"Don't cut off
your nose to spite your face."

Logic—"Because I said so."

Math—"I'm going to give you until the count of three: one... two..."

Probability—"You're going to be late for school if you don't leave now."

Recycling—"I'll find you a new home if you don't behave!"

Performance art—"I feel like I'm talking to a brick wall."

66

WHAT DO GIRLS DO WHO
HAVEN'T ANY MOTHERS
TO HELP THEM THROUGH
THEIR **TROUBLES?**

- LOUISA MAY ALCOTT -

99

A MOTHER HOLDS HER
CHILD'S HANDS FOR A
WHILE, BUT HOLDS THEIR
HEART FOREVER.

- ANONYMOUS -

A MOTHER'S HUG IS LIKE
A WARM CUP OF TEA
ON A RAINY DAY.

Biology is the least of what makes someone a mother.

- OPRAH WINFREY -

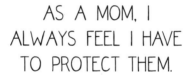

AS A MOM, I
ALWAYS FEEL I HAVE
TO PROTECT THEM.

- JAMI GERTZ ON HER CHILDREN -

THE PATIENCE OF
A MOTHER MIGHT BE
LIKENED TO A TUBE
OF TOOTHPASTE—
IT'S NEVER QUITE
ALL GONE.

- ANONYMOUS -

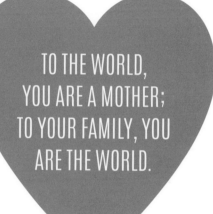

TO THE WORLD,
YOU ARE A MOTHER;
TO YOUR FAMILY, YOU
ARE THE WORLD.

NO ONE BUT A
WOMAN KNOWS
HOW TO SAY
**THINGS THAT ARE
AT ONCE GENTLE
AND DEEP.**

- VICTOR HUGO -

"

SHE WAS OF THE STUFF
OF WHICH GREAT MEN'S
MOTHERS ARE MADE.
SHE WAS... HATED AT
TEA PARTIES, FEARED
IN SHOPS, AND LOVED
AT CRISES.

- THOMAS HARDY -

NO INFLUENCE IS SO
POWERFUL AS THAT
OF THE MOTHER.

- SARAH JOSEPHA HALE -

My mother's great...
She could stop you from
doing anything, through
a closed door even,
with a single look.

- WHOOPI GOLDBERG -

YOU ALWAYS LIFT
MY SPIRITS.

YOUTH FADES; LOVE
DROOPS; THE LEAVES
OF FRIENDSHIP FALL; A
MOTHER'S SECRET HOPE
OUTLIVES THEM ALL.

- OLIVER WENDELL HOLMES, SR. -

A SMART
MOTHER MAKES
OFTEN A BETTER
DIAGNOSIS THAN A
POOR DOCTOR.

- AUGUST BIER -

A mother's arms are more comforting than anyone else's.

- DIANA, PRINCESS OF WALES -

SECRET SKILLS THAT ONLY MOMS KNOW:

How to speak Baby

How to get everyone washed, dressed, and out of the house before 9 a.m.

How to mend toys, clothes, and broken hearts

A CHILD'S FIRST TEACHER IS ITS MOTHER.

- PENG LIYUAN -

I KNOW ENOUGH TO
KNOW THAT WHEN
YOU'RE IN A PICKLE...
CALL MOM.

- JENNIFER GARNER -

TO A CHILD'S EAR,
"MOTHER" IS MAGIC IN
ANY LANGUAGE.

- ARLENE BENEDICT -

PARADISE IS AT THE FEET OF **THE MOTHER.**

- ARABIC PROVERB -

YOU ARE
IRREPLACEABLE.

I WILL ACCEPT LOTS OF THINGS, BUT NOT WHEN SOMEONE INSULTS MY MOM, THE NICEST PERSON IN THE WORLD.

- ANDY MURRAY -

THE TERM
"WORKING MOTHER"
IS RIDICULOUSLY
REDUNDANT.

- DONNA REED -

The only mothers it is safe to forget on Mother's Day are the good ones.

- MIGNON McLAUGHLIN -

SHE NEVER QUITE
LEAVES HER CHILDREN
AT HOME, EVEN
WHEN SHE DOESN'T
TAKE THEM ALONG.

- MARGARET CULKIN BANNING -

The most beautiful
word on the lips of
mankind is the
word "mother."

- KAHLIL GIBRAN -

66

THERE IS ONLY ONE PRETTY CHILD IN THE WORLD, AND EVERY MOTHER HAS IT.

- CHINESE PROVERB -

THINK OF YOUR
MOTHER AND SMILE
FOR ALL OF THE GOOD
PRECIOUS MOMENTS.

- ANA MONNAR -

WHILE WE TRY TO
TEACH OUR CHILDREN
ABOUT LIFE, OUR
CHILDREN TEACH
US WHAT LIFE IS
ALL ABOUT.

- ANGELA SCHWINDT -

THANK YOU FOR
THE EXAMPLE YOU
SET ME EVERY DAY.

MOTHERS
ALWAYS KNOW.

- OPRAH WINFREY -

MOTHERHOOD IS NOT FOR THE FAINT-HEARTED.

FROGS, SKINNED KNEES, AND THE INSULTS OF TEENAGE GIRLS ARE NOT MEANT FOR THE WIMPY.

- DANIELLE STEEL -

AWARDS FOR THE
BEST MOM EVER:

Culinary Genius

Bravery in the Face
of Gross Things

Queen of Solutions

Extraordinary Alertness
After a Night of No Sleep

Best Hand-Holder

MOTHERS... CARRY THE
KEY OF OUR SOULS
IN THEIR BOSOMS.

- OLIVER WENDELL HOLMES, SR. -

SING OUT LOUD IN
THE CAR EVEN, OR
ESPECIALLY, IF IT
EMBARRASSES
YOUR CHILDREN.

- MARILYN PENLAND -

Sometimes the strength
of motherhood is greater
than natural laws.

- BARBARA KINGSOLVER -

MOM, YOU'RE MY
FAVORITE PERSON.

"

NO PAINTER'S BRUSH,
NOR POET'S PEN, IN
JUSTICE TO HER FAME,
HAS EVER REACHED
HALF HIGH ENOUGH
TO WRITE A
MOTHER'S NAME.

- ANONYMOUS -

CHILDREN KEEP US IN CHECK. THEIR LAUGHTER PREVENTS OUR HEARTS FROM HARDENING.

- QUEEN RANIA OF JORDAN -

SOME MOTHERS ARE
KISSING MOTHERS AND
SOME ARE SCOLDING
MOTHERS, BUT IT
IS LOVE JUST THE
SAME, AND MOST
MOTHERS KISS AND
SCOLD TOGETHER.

- PEARL S. BUCK -

SILENCE IS GOLDEN,
UNLESS YOU HAVE KIDS;
THEN SILENCE
IS SUSPICIOUS.

When you look at your
mother, you are looking
at the purest love you
will ever know.

- MITCH ALBOM -

CHILD-REARING MYTH #1:
LABOR ENDS WHEN
THE BABY IS BORN.

- ANONYMOUS -

THE MOMENT A CHILD IS BORN, THE MOTHER IS ALSO BORN.

- BHAGWAN SHREE RAJNEESH -

I AM LUCKY TO HAVE
A MOM WITH SUCH
A GREAT SENSE
OF HUMOR.

A MOTHER IS SHE
WHO CAN TAKE
THE PLACE OF ALL
OTHERS BUT WHOSE
PLACE NO ONE
ELSE CAN TAKE.

- GASPARD MERMILLOD -

THERE ARE ONLY TWO
THINGS A CHILD WILL
SHARE WILLINGLY:
COMMUNICABLE
DISEASES AND HIS
MOTHER'S AGE.

- BENJAMIN SPOCK -

THINGS IN MOM'S HANDBAG:

Hand sanitizer

Spare pair of socks

A seemingly endless supply
of tissues and band aids

Emergency chocolate supplies

Safety pins

Factor-50 sunscreen

Foldable waterproof jacket

A notebook and lots of
pens and pencils

MOTHER IS THE
ONE WE COUNT ON
FOR THE THINGS
THAT MATTER
MOST OF ALL.

- KATHARINE BUTLER HATHAWAY -

Motherhood in all its guises and permutations is more art than science.

- MELINDA M. MARSHALL -

I CAN DO ANYTHING
BECAUSE I'VE GOT
YOU BY MY SIDE.

A MOTHER IS NOT
A PERSON TO LEAN
ON, BUT A PERSON
TO MAKE LEANING
UNNECESSARY.

- DOROTHY CANFIELD FISHER -

MOST MOTHERS
ARE INSTINCTIVE
PHILOSOPHERS.

- HARRIET BEECHER STOWE -

Children are the anchors that hold a mother to life.

- SOPHOCLES -

NINETY PERCENT OF
PARENTING IS THINKING
ABOUT WHEN YOU CAN
LIE DOWN AGAIN.

"

I THINK MY LIFE BEGAN WITH WAKING UP AND LOVING MY MOTHER'S **FACE.**

- GEORGE ELIOT -

"

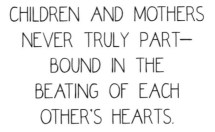

CHILDREN AND MOTHERS
NEVER TRULY PART—
BOUND IN THE
BEATING OF EACH
OTHER'S HEARTS.

- CHARLOTTE GRAY -

A SUBURBAN
MOTHER'S ROLE
IS TO DELIVER
CHILDREN
**OBSTETRICALLY
ONCE, AND BY CAR
FOREVER AFTER.**

- PETER DE VRIES -

OUT OF ALL THE
REST, MY MOM
IS THE BEST.

WORKING MOTHERS
ARE GUINEA PIGS
IN A SCIENTIFIC
EXPERIMENT TO
SHOW THAT SLEEP
IS NOT NECESSARY
TO HUMAN LIFE.

- ANONYMOUS -

66

THERE'S NOTHING LIKE A MAMA-HUG.

- TERRI GUILLEMETS -

NO LANGUAGE
CAN EXPRESS THE
POWER AND BEAUTY
AND HEROISM AND
MAJESTY OF A
MOTHER'S LOVE.

- EDWIN HUBBELL CHAPIN -

She may scold you for little things, but never for the big ones.

– HARRY S. TRUMAN –

MOMS HAVE THE BEST
PATIENCE, EVEN WHEN
THEIR KIDS...

... come home covered in
mud from head to toe

... leave their wet towels in a
heap on the bathroom floor

... forget that it's their turn
to empty the dishwasher

... never remember to turn the
lights off when leaving a room

... drink orange juice
from the carton

A FATHER'S
GOODNESS IS
HIGHER THAN
THE MOUNTAINS;
A MOTHER'S
GOODNESS IS
DEEPER THAN
THE SEA.

- JAPANESE PROVERB -

THE HEART OF
A MOTHER IS A
DEEP ABYSS AT
THE BOTTOM OF
**WHICH YOU WILL
ALWAYS FIND
FORGIVENESS.**

- HONORÉ DE BALZAC -

66

WHATEVER ELSE IS UNSURE IN THIS STINKING DUNGHILL OF A WORLD A MOTHER'S LOVE IS NOT.

- JAMES JOYCE -

99

MOM, I DON'T KNOW WHAT I'D DO WITHOUT YOU.

**Parenthood:
the state of being
better chaperoned
than you were
before marriage.**

- MARCELENE COX -

YOU WILL ALWAYS
BE YOUR CHILD'S
FAVORITE TOY.

- VICKI LANSKY -

YOU'RE THE BEST
MOM BECAUSE...

... you take me shopping
until I've found exactly
the right thing to wear

... you always tell me I can do it

... you listen to all my stories—
and you remember them

... you know just how
to cheer me up

... you have taught me so
many valuable life lessons

EVERY HOME IS
A UNIVERSITY AND
THE PARENTS ARE
THE TEACHERS.

- MAHATMA GANDHI -

ONLY MOTHERS
CAN THINK OF THE
FUTURE—BECAUSE THEY
GIVE BIRTH TO IT
IN THEIR CHILDREN.

- MAXIM GORKY -

YOU NEVER LET
ME DOWN.

THERE WAS NEVER A
GREAT MAN WHO HAD
NOT A GREAT MOTHER.

- OLIVE SCHREINER -

MY FAVORITE THING
ABOUT BEING A MOM
IS JUST WHAT A
BETTER PERSON IT
MAKES YOU ON A
DAILY BASIS.

- DREW BARRYMORE -

The hand that rocks the cradle usually is attached to someone who isn't getting enough sleep.

- JOHN FIEBIG -

MOTHER IS THE
HEARTBEAT IN THE
HOME; AND WITHOUT
HER, THERE SEEMS TO
BE NO HEART THROB.

- LEROY BROWNLOW -

YOU GIVE THE
BEST ADVICE.

"A MOTHER IS THE TRUEST FRIEND WE HAVE.

- WASHINGTON IRVING -

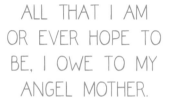

ALL THAT I AM
OR EVER HOPE TO
BE, I OWE TO MY
ANGEL MOTHER.

- ABRAHAM LINCOLN -

A little girl, asked where
her home was, replied,
"Where mother is."

- KEITH L. BROOKS -

THANK YOU FOR BEING...

... MOM IN A MILLION!